FIRST GRAPHICS | BODY SYSTEMS

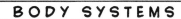

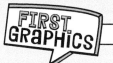

A Tour of Your Digestive System

by Molly Kolpin
illustrated by Chris B. Jones

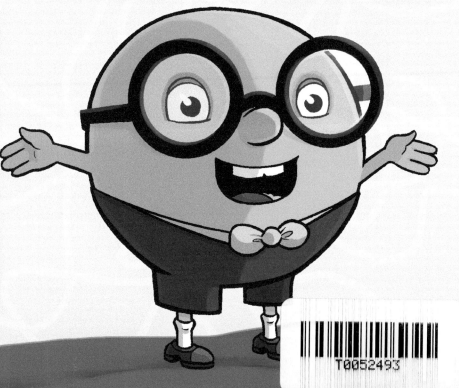

CONSULTANT:
MARJORIE J. HOGAN, MD
ASSOCIATE PROFESSOR OF PEDIATRICS AND PEDIATRICIAN
UNIVERSITY OF MINNESOTA AND HENNEPIN COUNTY MEDICAL CENTER
MINNEAPOLIS, MINNESOTA

CAPSTONE PRESS
a capstone imprint

First Graphics are published by Capstone Press,
1710 Roe Crest Drive, North Mankato, Minnesota 56003.
www.capstonepub.com

Library of Congress Cataloging-in-Publication Data
Kolpin, Molly.
A tour of your digestive system / by Molly Kolpin ; illustrated by Chris B. Jones.
p. cm.—(First graphics. Body systems)
Summary: "In graphic novel format, follows Peter Pea as he travels through and
explains the workings of the human digestive system"—Provided by publisher.
Includes bibliographical references and index.
ISBN 978-1-4296-8430-9 (library binding)
ISBN 978-1-4296-9324-0 (paperback)
ISBN 978-1-62065-262-6 (ebook PDF)
1. Digestion—Juvenile literature. 2. Digestive organs—Juvenile literature. I. Jones,
Chris B., ill. II. Title.
QP145.K65 2013
612.3—dc23
2011051826

Editor: Christopher L. Harbo
Designer: Lori Bye
Art Director: Nathan Gassman
Production Specialist: Kathy McColley

Printed in the United States   5657

Table of Contents

Diving into Digestion

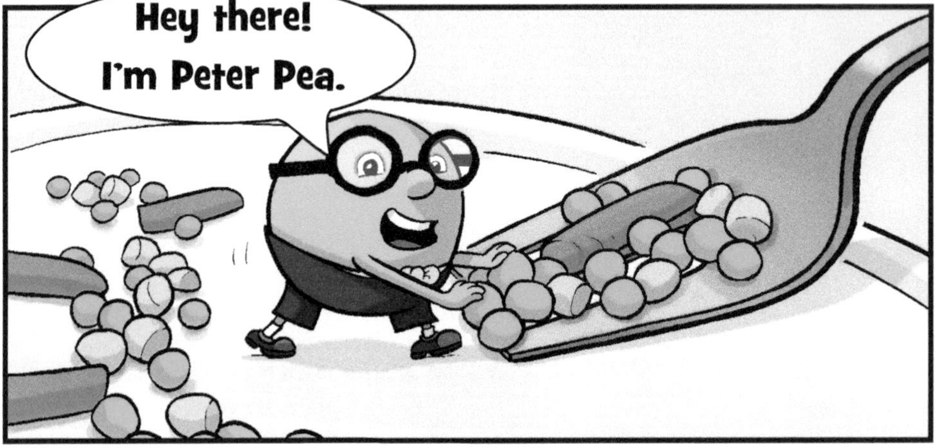
Hey there!
I'm Peter Pea.

You're just in time for a wild ride inside the human body.

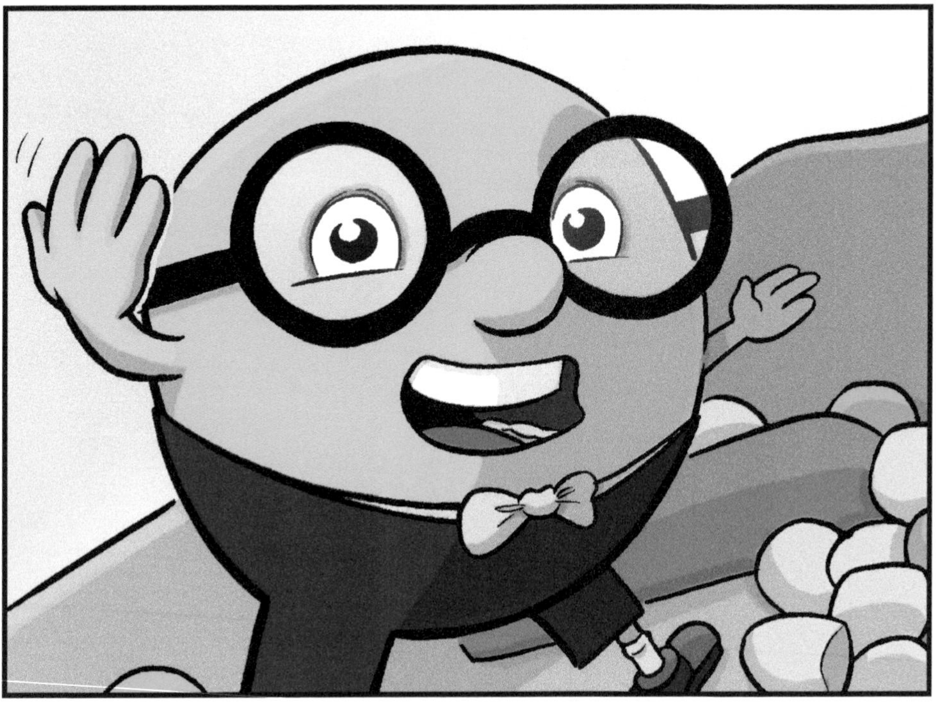

Join me as I travel through the digestive system!

The digestive system is made up of connected tubes. Food travels through these tubes.

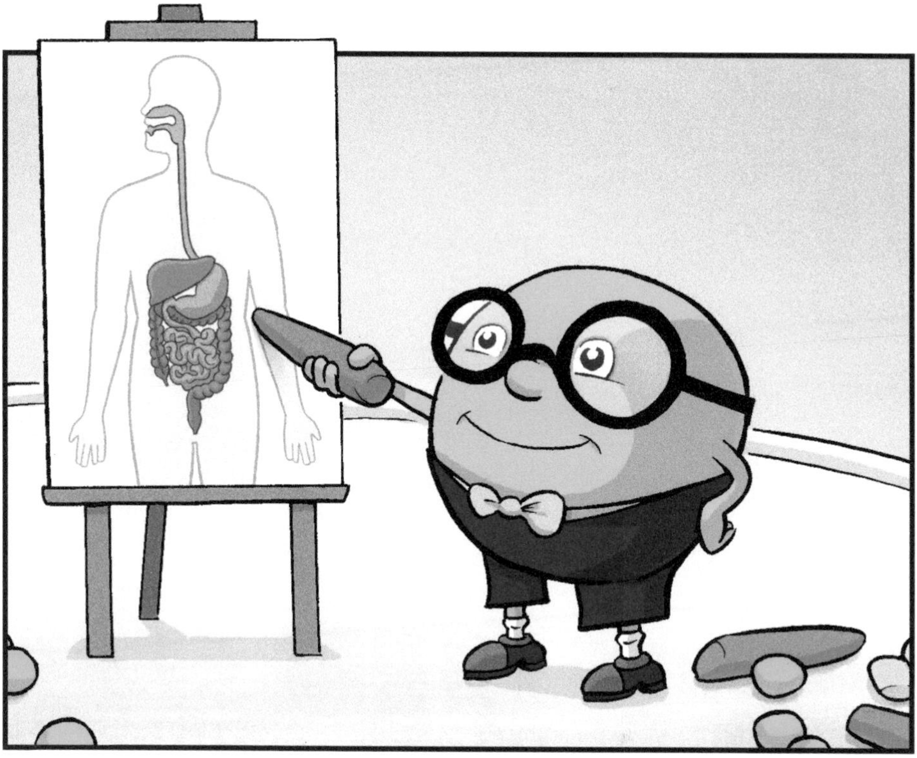

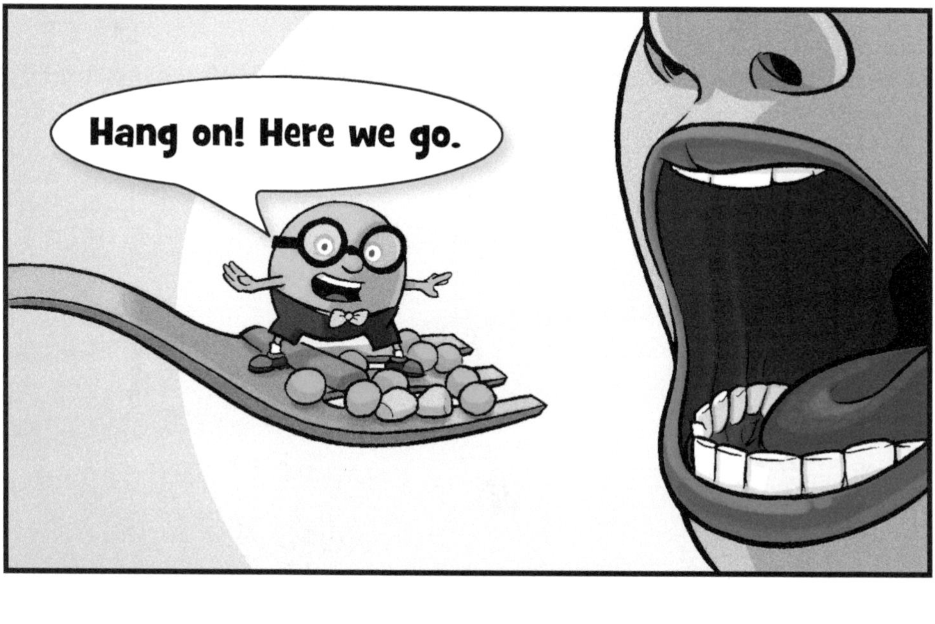
Hang on! Here we go.

Digestion turns food into energy.

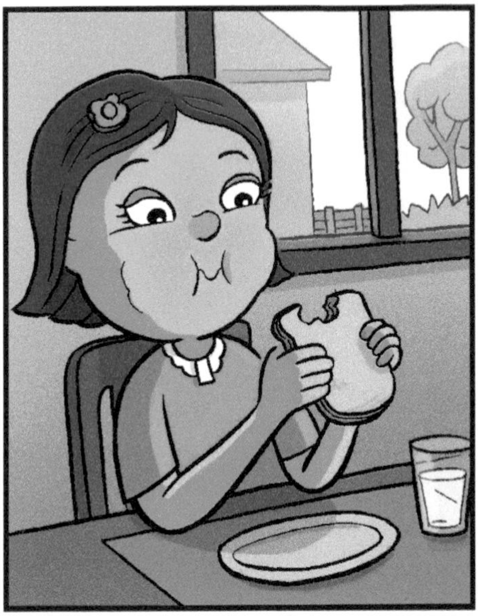

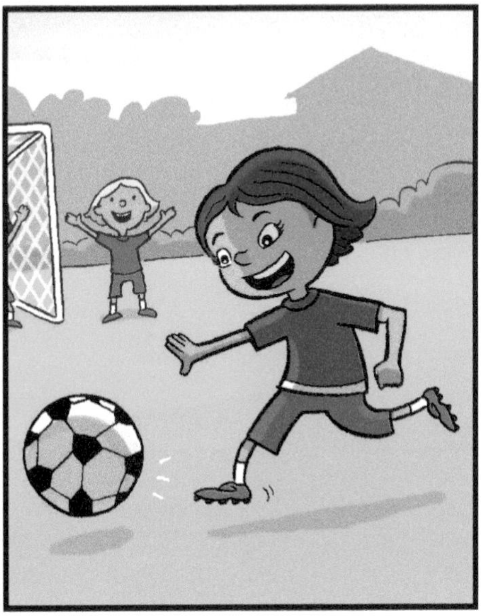

It begins in the mouth.

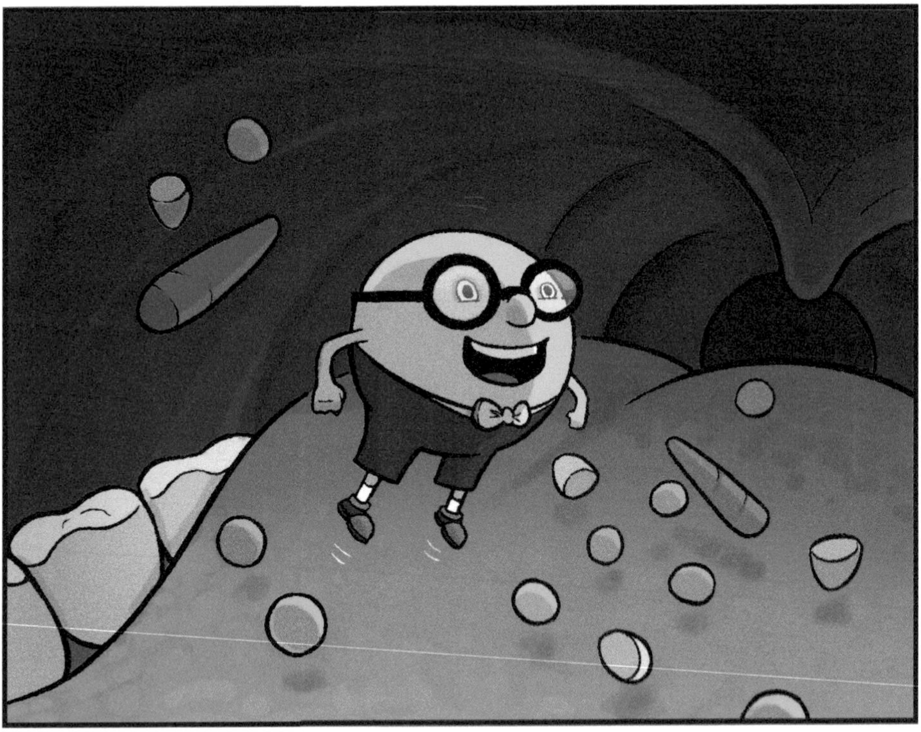

Saliva makes food soft. Teeth crush food into small pieces.

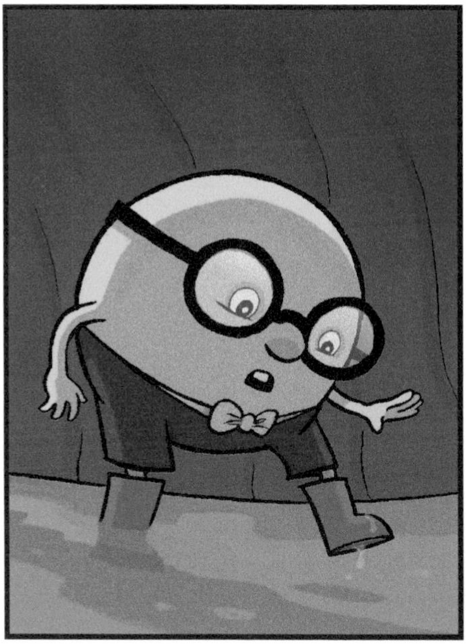

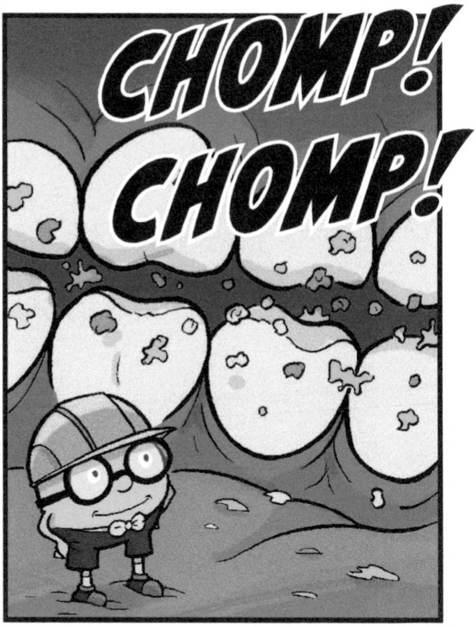
CHOMP!
CHOMP!

Finally, the tongue pushes food to the back of the mouth to be swallowed.

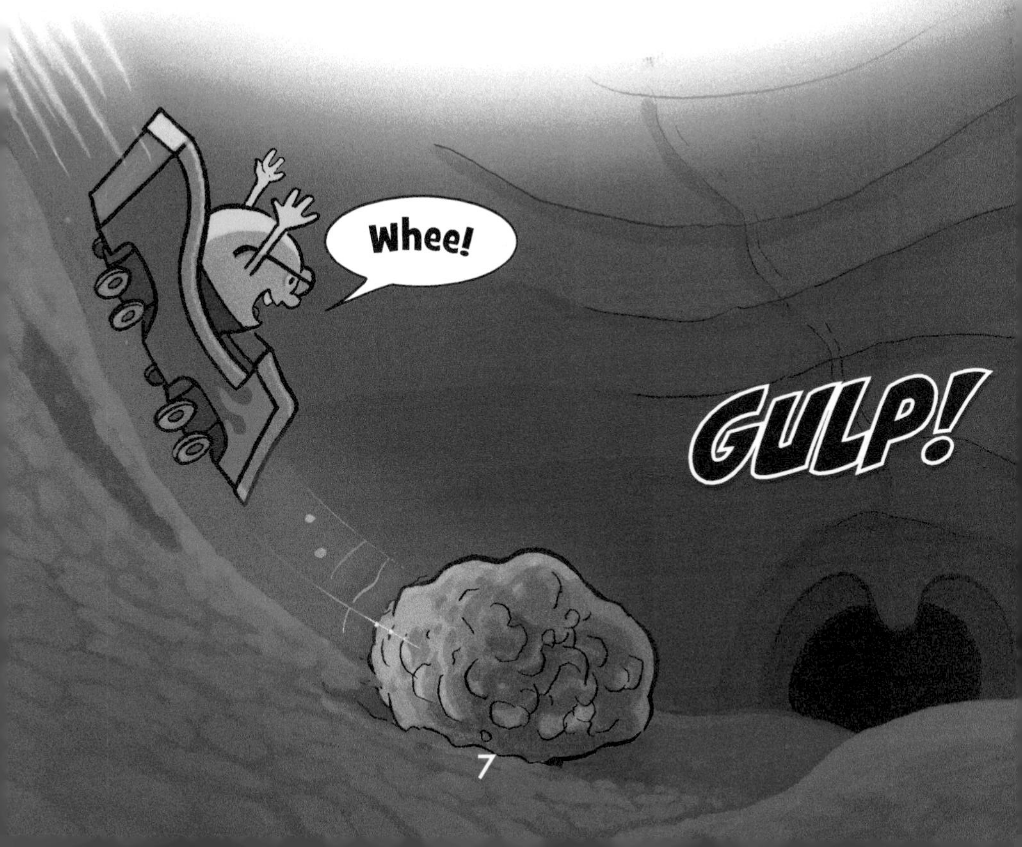
Whee!
GULP!

After being swallowed, food moves down the esophagus.

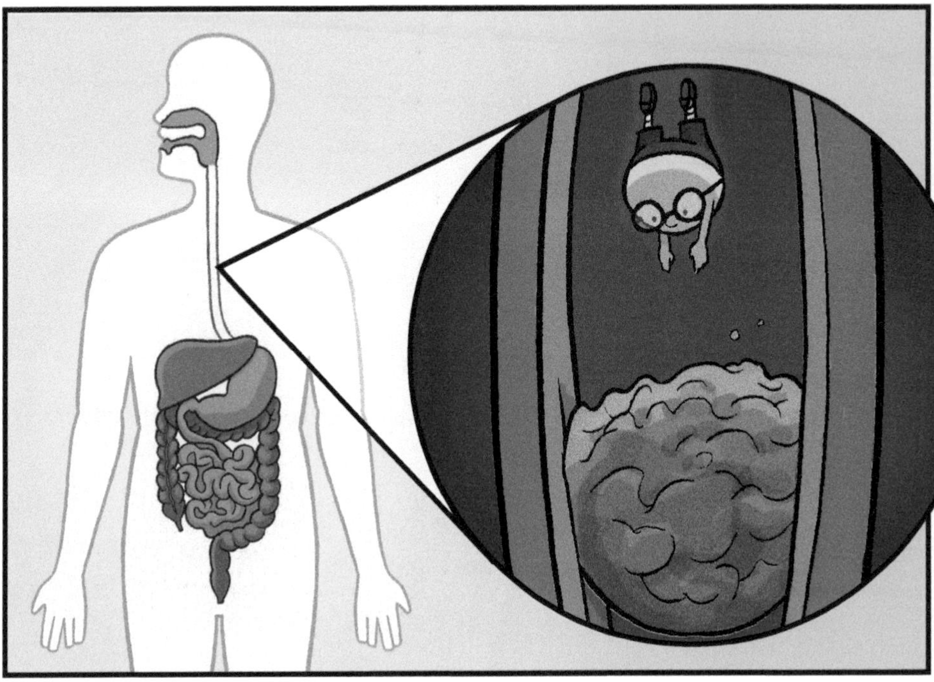

The esophagus is a stretchy tube. It connects the mouth and stomach.

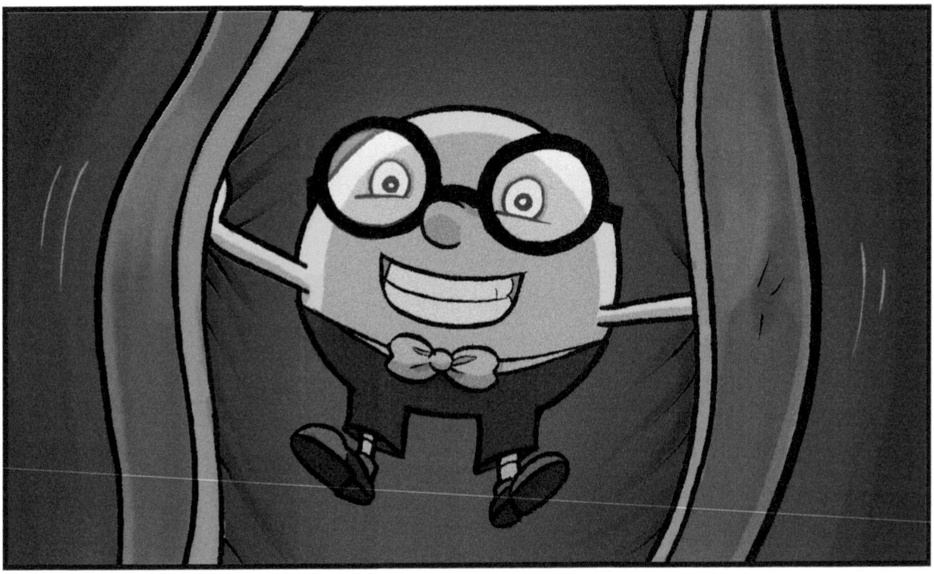

Muscles slowly squeeze food through the tube.

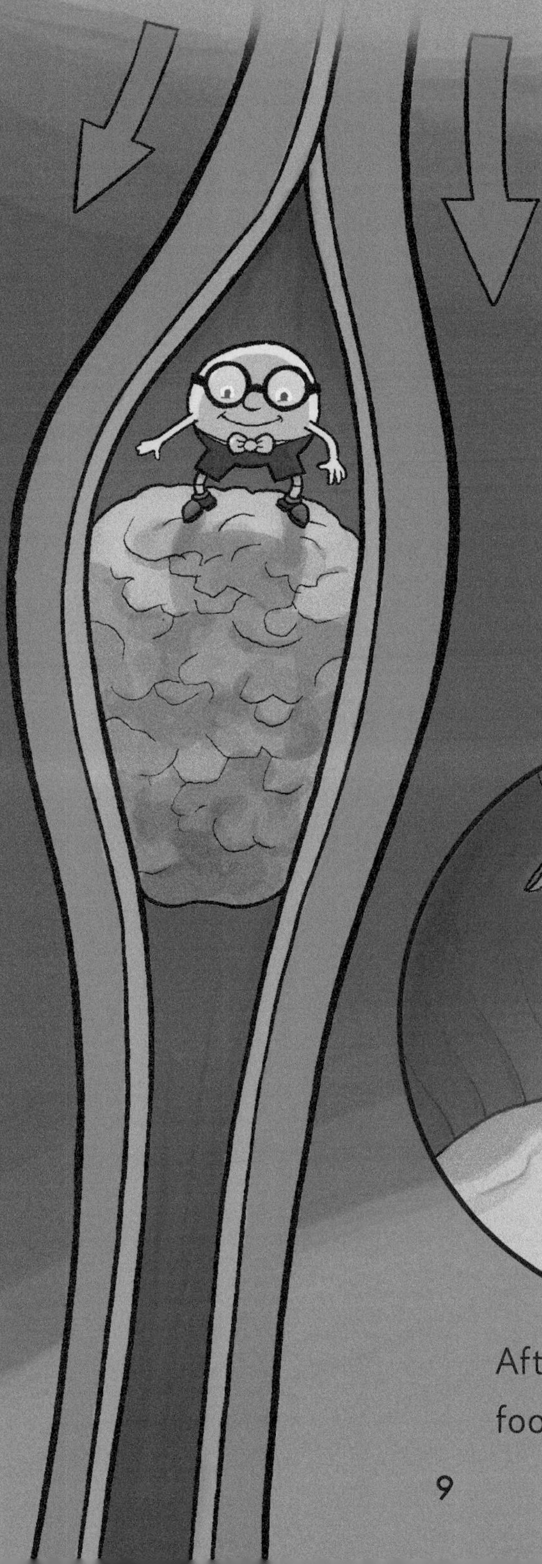

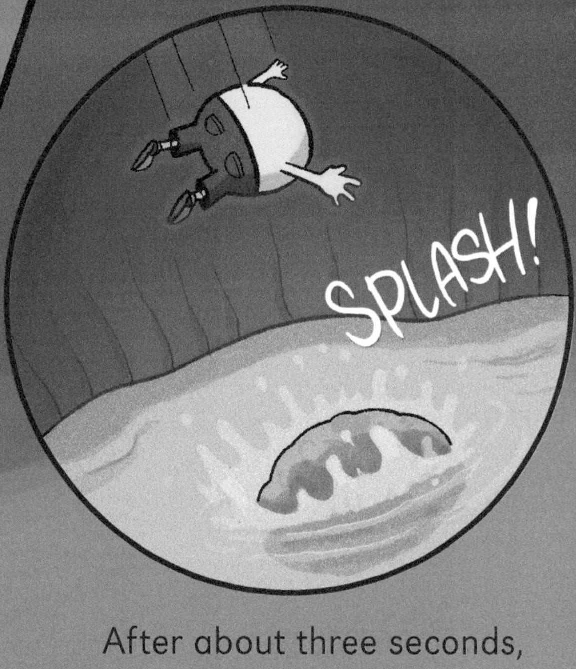
SPLASH!

After about three seconds, food lands in the stomach.

Stopping by the Stomach

The stomach is a stretchy sack.

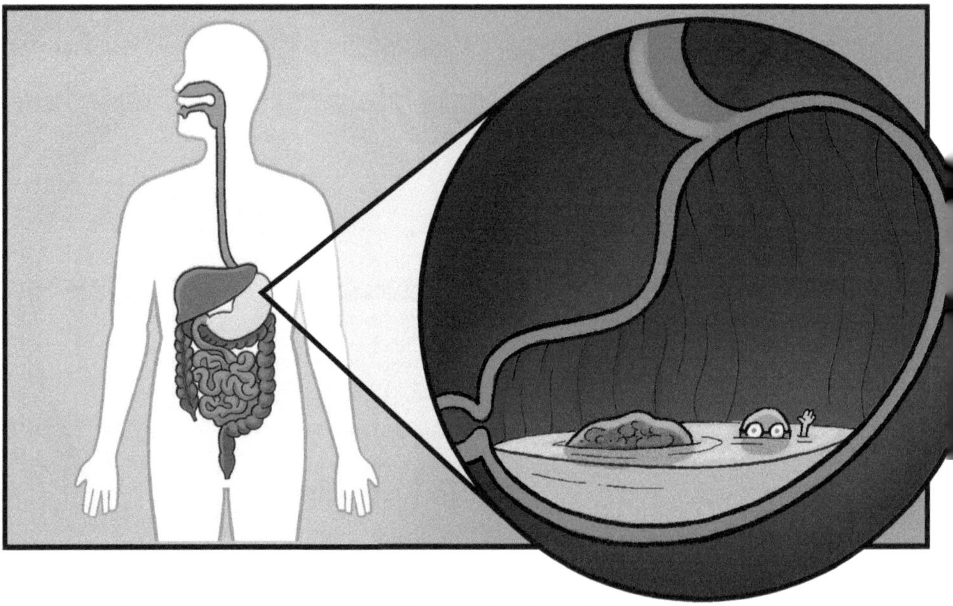

Stomach muscles mix and mash food into small pieces.

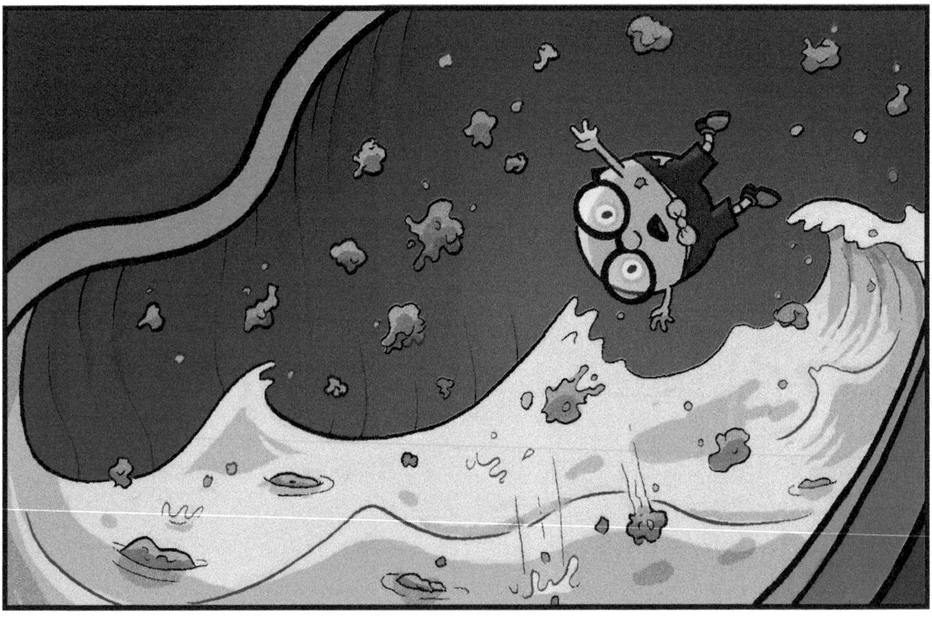

Stomach juices turn food into a chunky slush.

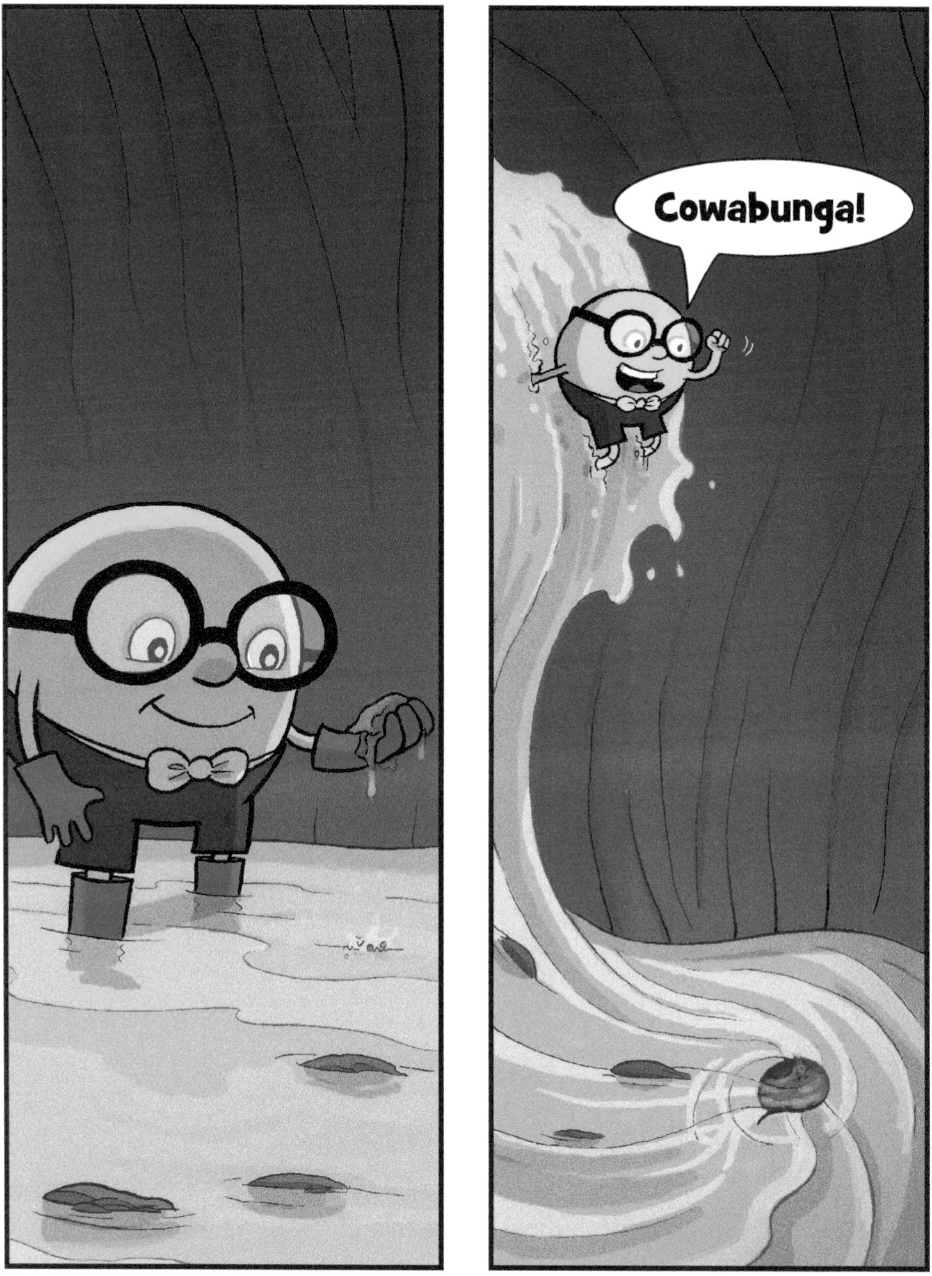
Cowabunga!

Then a valve opens to let the slush flow into the small intestine.

Going with Your Gut

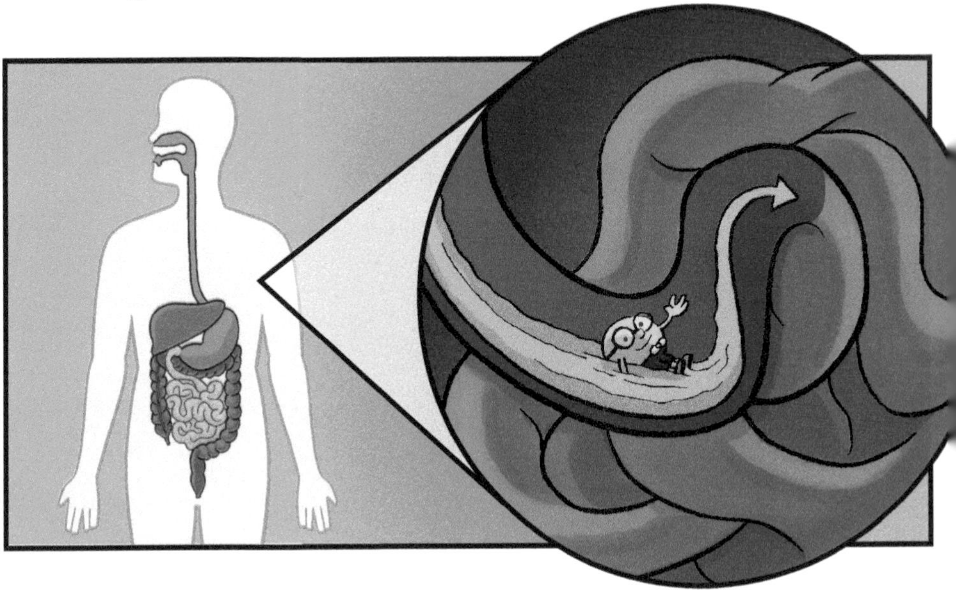

The small intestine is a skinny tube crammed beneath the stomach.

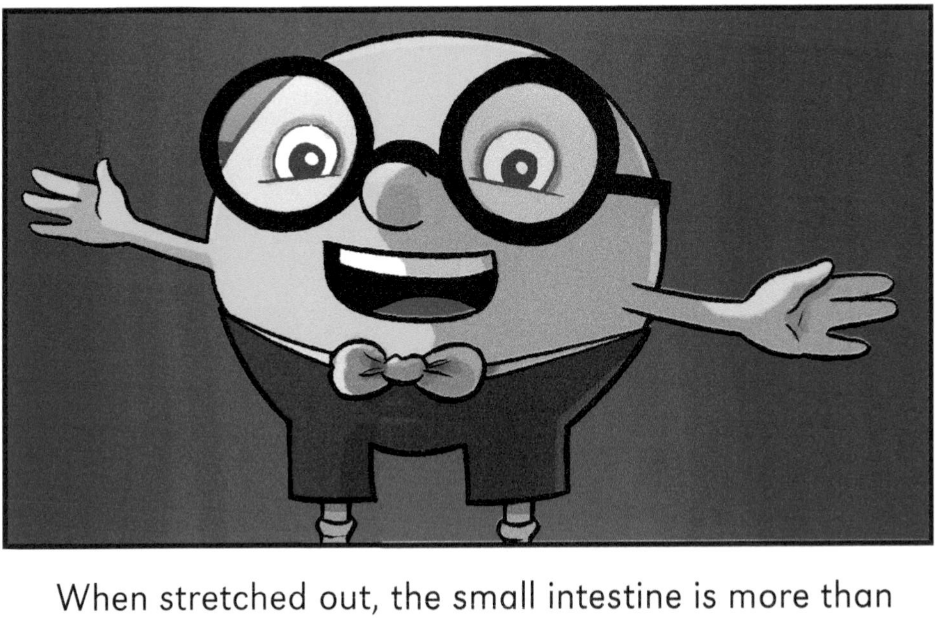

When stretched out, the small intestine is more than 20 feet (6 meters) long!

The small intestine grinds food.

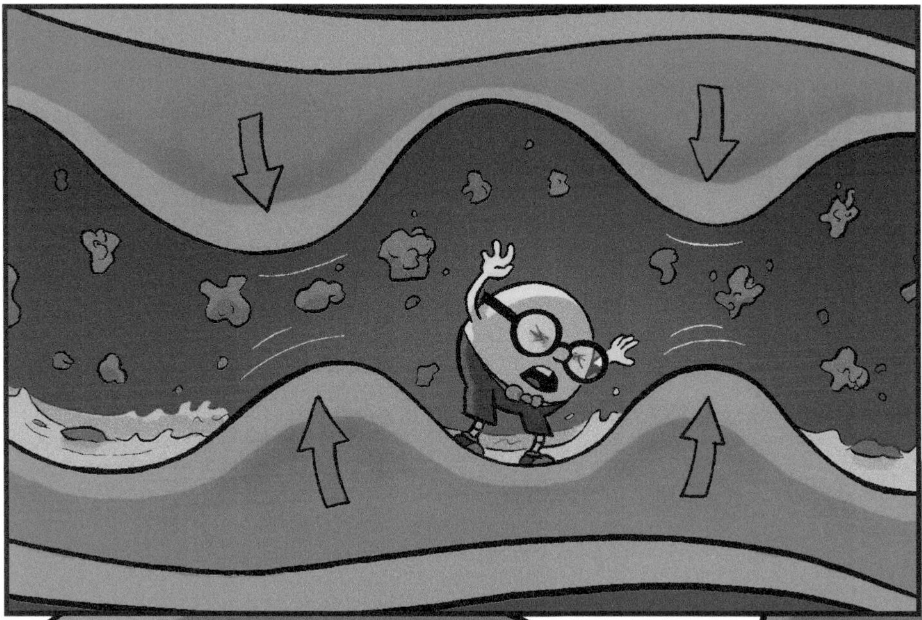

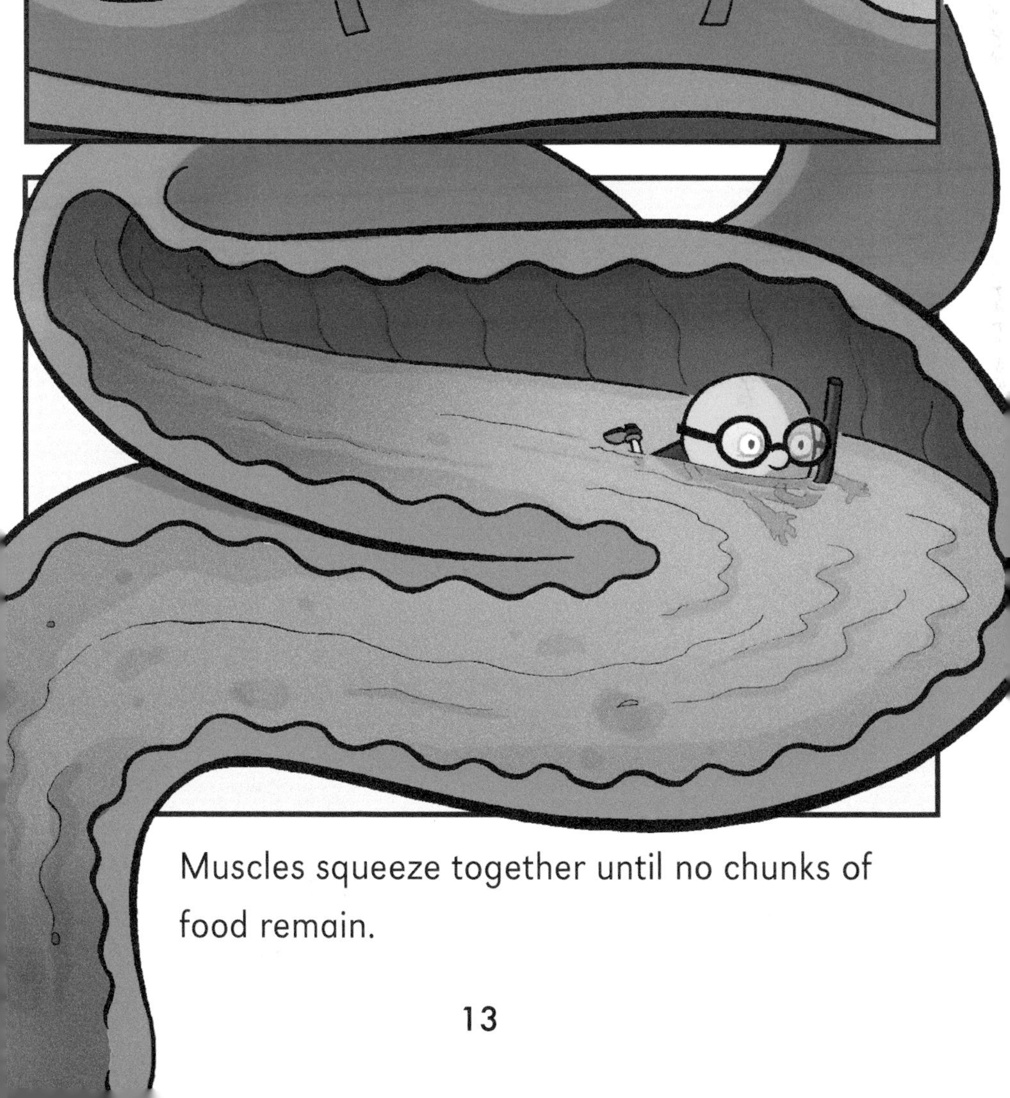

Muscles squeeze together until no chunks of food remain.

The small intestine also holds food while other organs help with digestion.

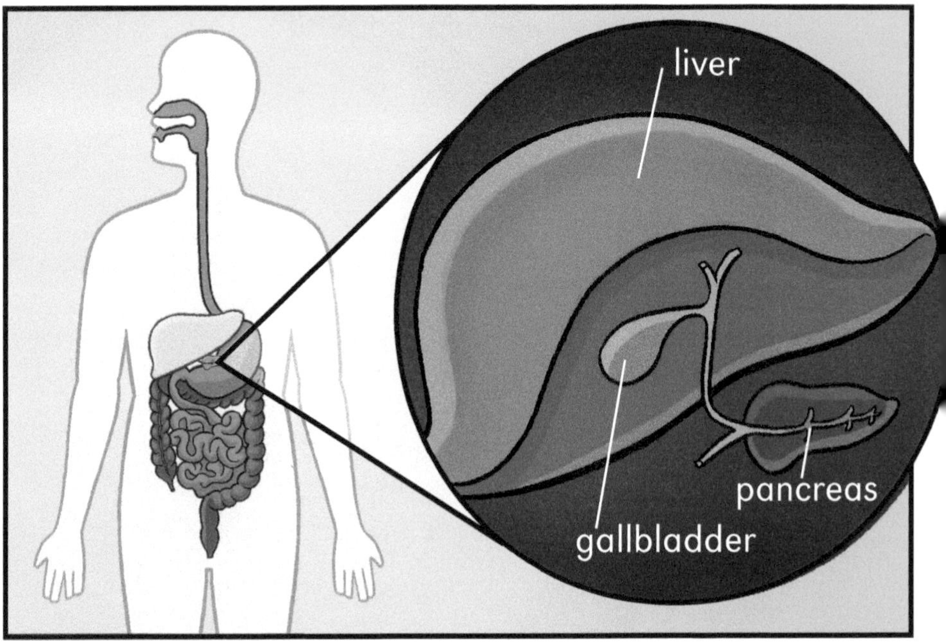
liver
pancreas
gallbladder

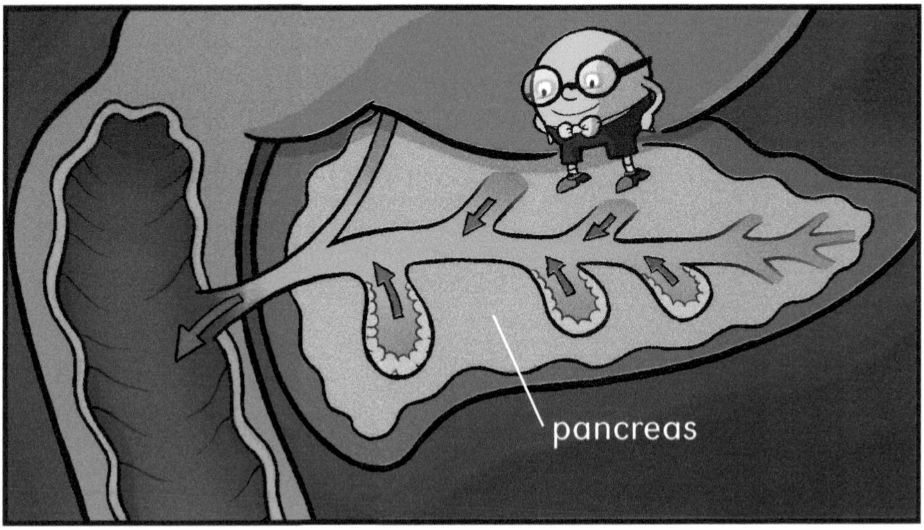
pancreas

The pancreas makes juice that breaks down fats and proteins.

The liver makes bile. This juice breaks down fats.

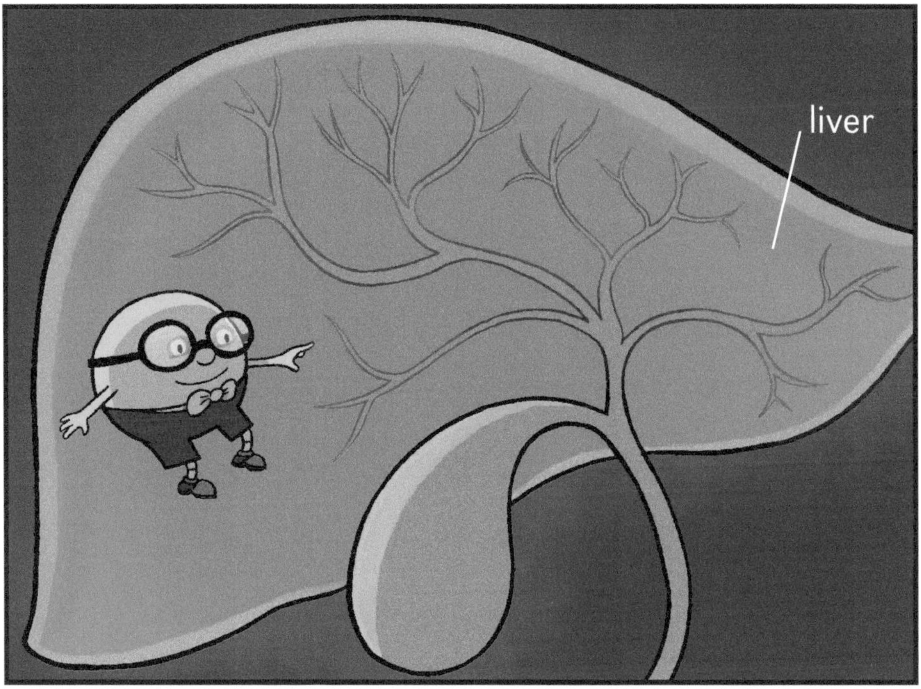
liver

The gallbladder stores bile.

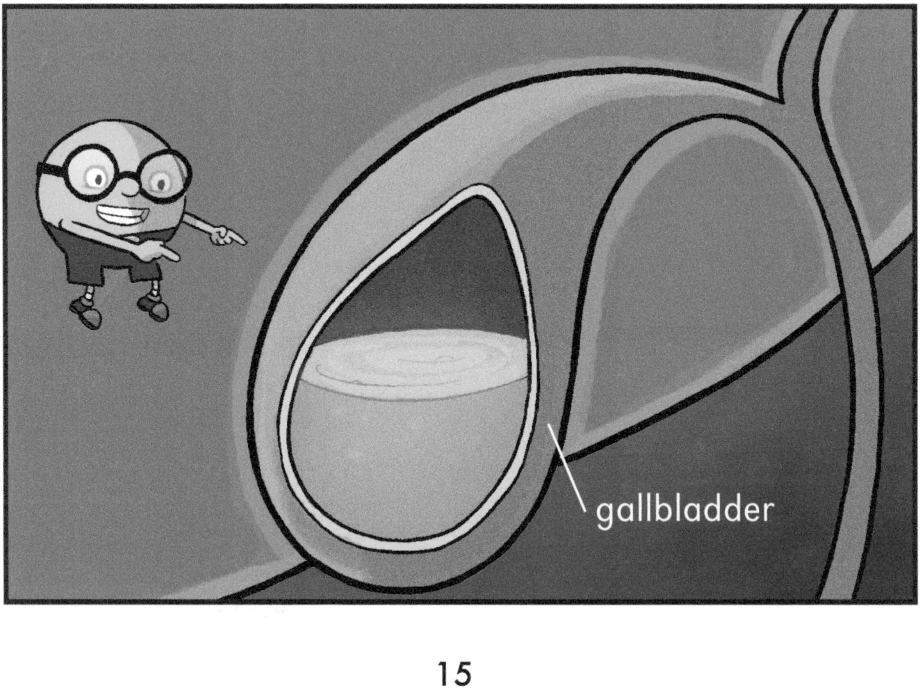
gallbladder

While food moves through the small intestine, nutrients pass through its walls.

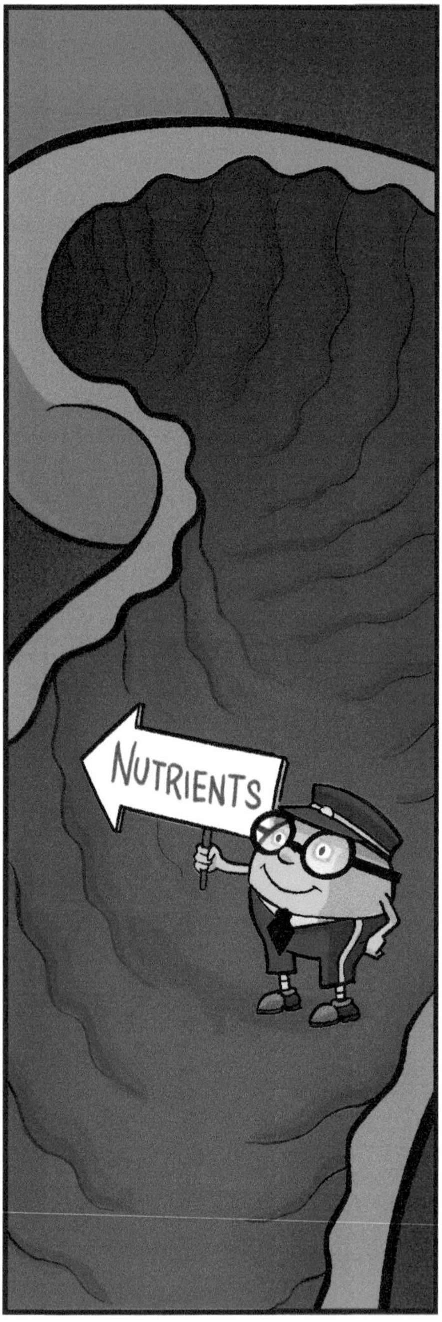
NUTRIENTS

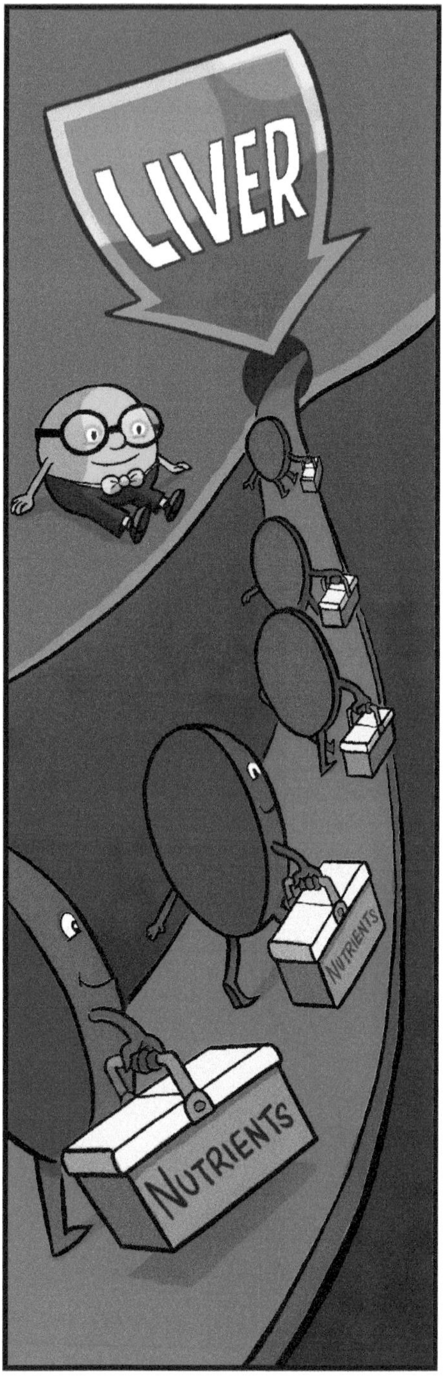
LIVER
NUTRIENTS
NUTRIENTS

Blood carries the nutrients to the liver.

The liver takes out harmful stuff. Then it releases the nutrients into the body.

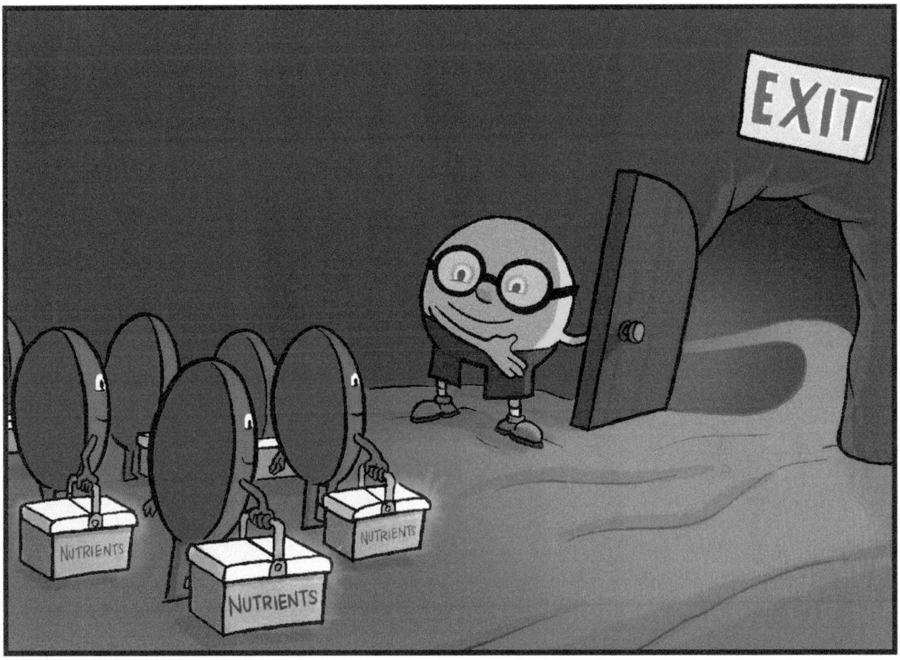
EXIT
NUTRIENTS
NUTRIENTS
NUTRIENTS

The liver also stores any extra nutrients.

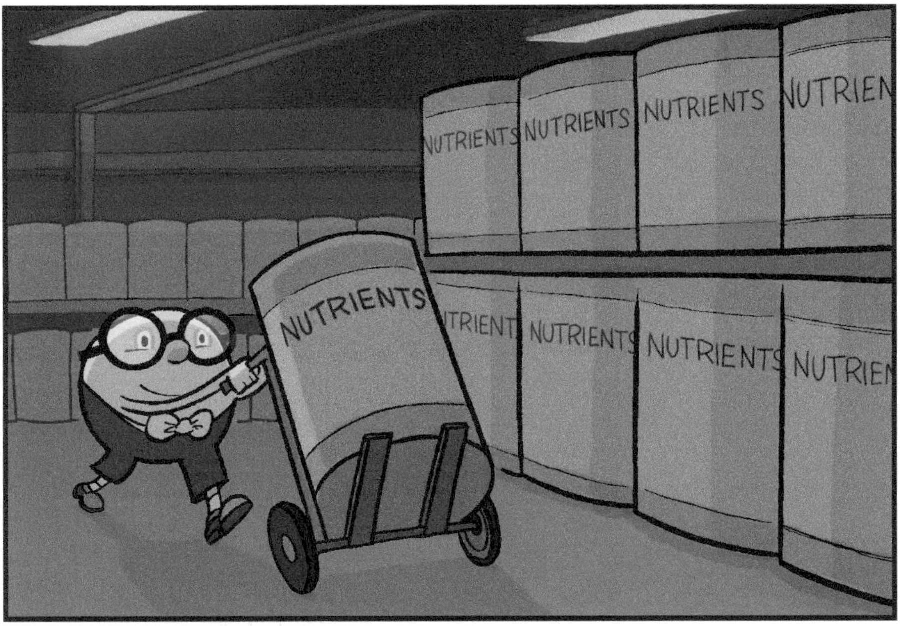
NUTRIENTS
NUTRIENTS
NUTRIENTS
NUTRIENTS
NUTRIENTS
NUTRIENTS

Finishing with a Flush

We've reached the last step in digestion. Time to get rid of the waste.

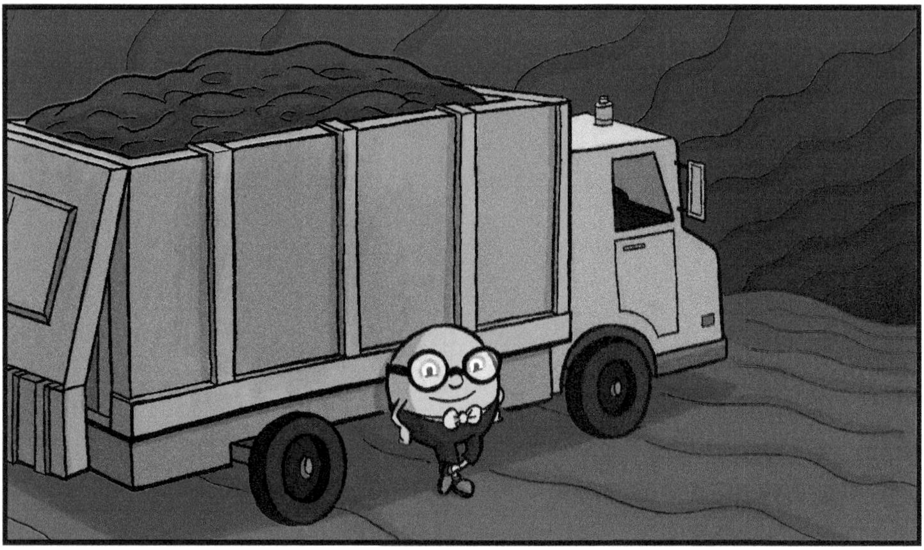

Waste moves from the small intestine into the large intestine.

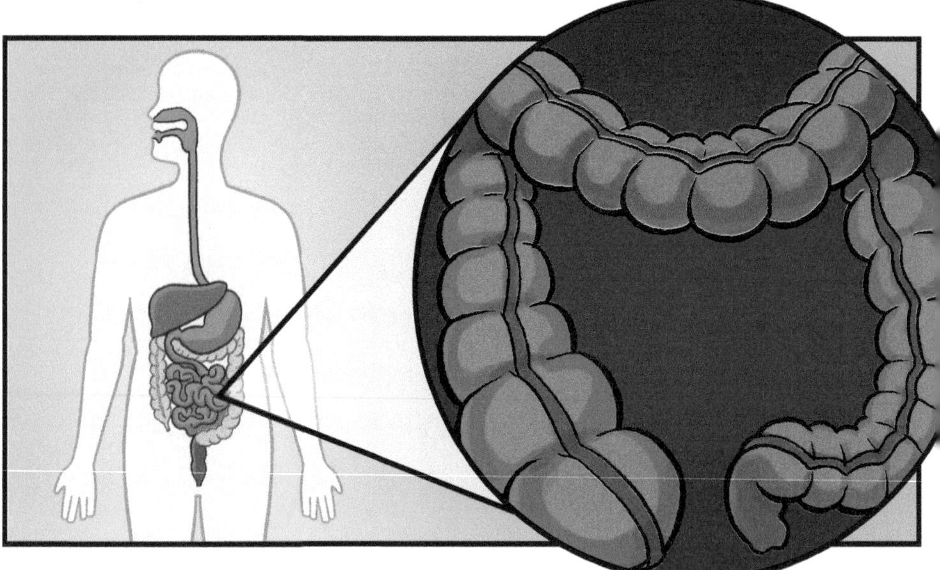

The large intestine is shorter than the small intestine. But it's twice as wide.

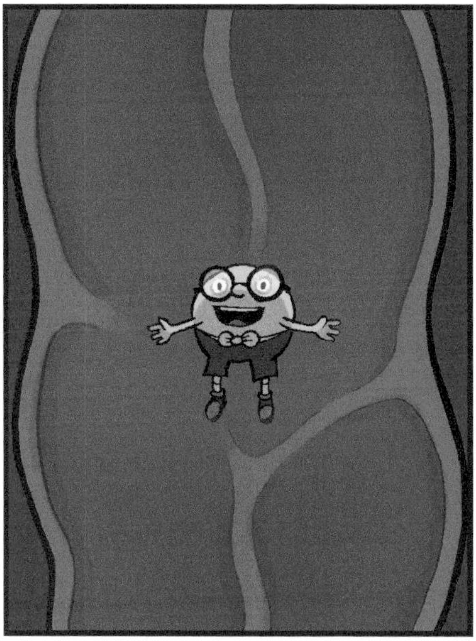

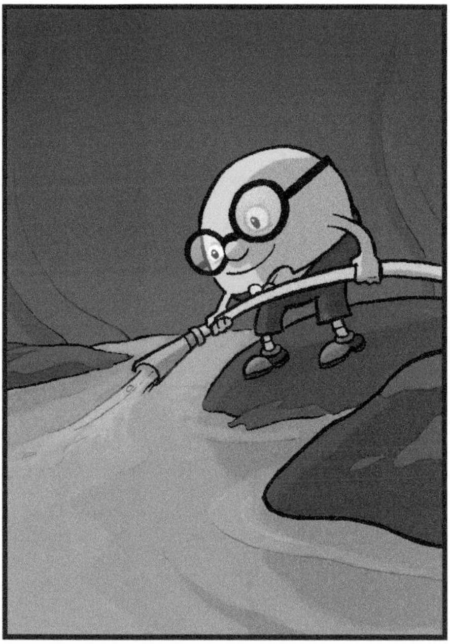

Inside the large intestine, water is sucked out of the waste.

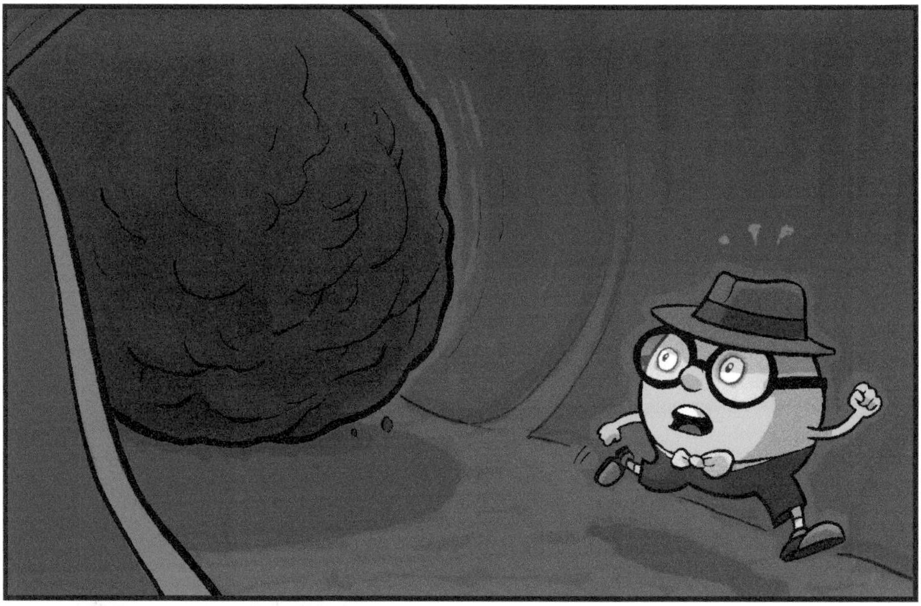

Slowly, the waste turns into a solid.

The waste moves from the large intestine to the rectum.

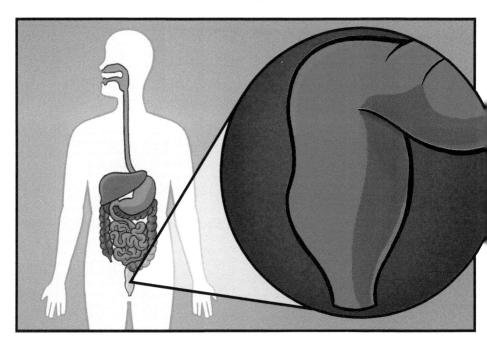

The rectum stores wastes until it's time to go to the bathroom. Then wastes leave the body.

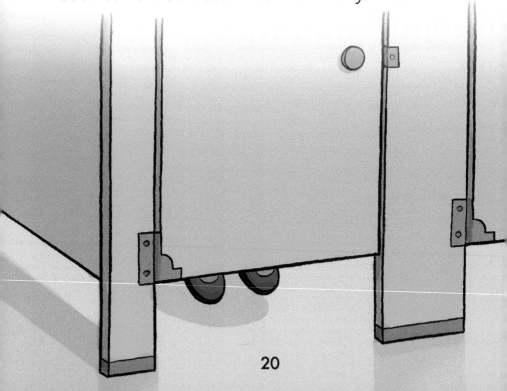

The body has taken nutrients from food. Now it has removed the leftover wastes too.

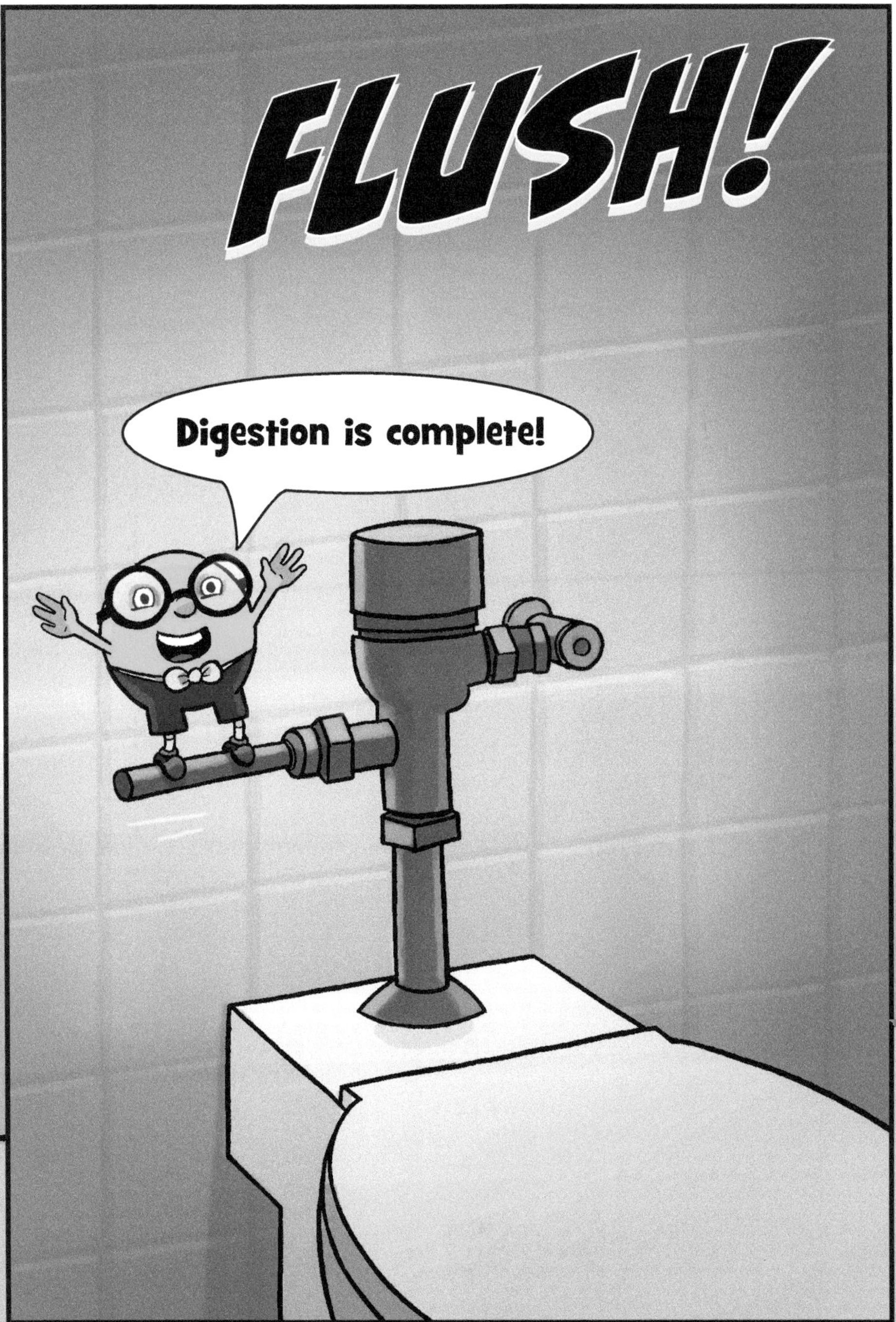
FLUSH!
Digestion is complete!

Glossary

bile—a green liquid that is made by the liver and helps digest food

energy—the strength to do active things without getting tired

nutrients—parts of food, such as vitamins, that are used for growth

organ—a body part that does a certain job

protein—a substance found in foods such as meat, cheese, eggs, and fish

saliva—the clear liquid in your mouth that helps you swallow and begin to digest food

valve—a movable part that controls the flow of liquid leaving the stomach

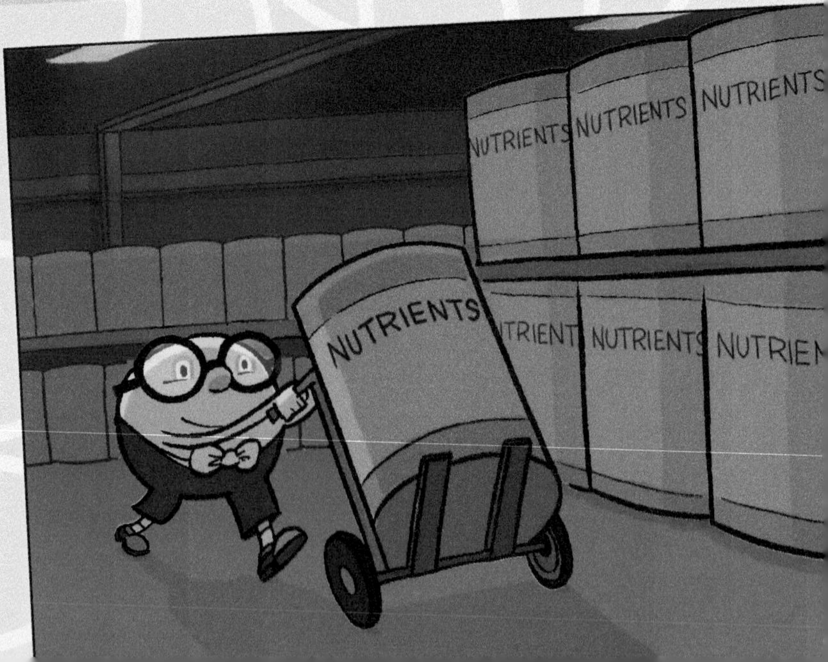
NUTRIENTS
NUTRIENTS
NUTRIENTS
NUTRIENTS

Read More

Johnson, Rebecca L. *Your Digestive System.* How Does Your Body Work? Minneapolis: Lerner Publications Co., 2013.

Jordan, Apple. *My Stomach.* My Body. New York: Marshall Cavendish Benchmark, 2012.

Thomas, Isabel. *Why Do I Burp?* Inside My Body. Chicago: Raintree, 2011.

Internet Sites

FactHound offers a safe, fun way to find Internet sites related to this book. All of the sites on FactHound have been researched by our staff.

Here's all you do:

Visit *www.facthound.com*

Type in this code: 9781429684309

Super-cool stuff!

Check out projects, games and lots more at
www.capstonekids.com

Index